Treasured Memories

PATIENCE STRONG

Frederick Muller Ltd
London

The Goblet of Life

Life is full of endings and of beginnings too.
Life is always passing, yet life is always new —
springing up replenished when winter's course
has run — Life, a brimming goblet of wine
warmed by the sun.

Life can never finish — It can only change —
into something different, wonderful and
strange . . . Nature points the lesson, Nature
gives the clue — when the hedges quicken and
the green thrusts through.

Make Me a Memory

Make me a memory — something to
treasure — after the glow and the
glamour have gone . . . like some old
melody — bringing back pleasure,
strangely and tenderly lingering on.

Say something wonderful — words I'll
remember — if Time in passing should
tear us apart . . . Life takes its course.
Love must burn to its ember. Say just
one thing I can hold in my heart.

Give me a day of delight and perfection
— with never a shadow, or pang of
regret — a day to recall with a loving
affection — to cherish for ever and
never forget.

The Adventurers

Dear, we'll have our problems, but we'll share them.
Love, we'll have our crosses, but we'll bear them. For
the best we'll always strive — Into the strongest
blizzard drive — to keep our nerve and keep alive —
together. Soon, please God, we'll see things looking
brighter — the load upon our shoulders growing

lighter. This the hope that day by day — will keep us plodding on our way — And we'll make it if we stay — together.

Sweetheart, let the cynics say we're crazy — to marry with tomorrow's view so hazy . . . I'd buy you the whole world if I could — I shan't. I can't. That's understood — but we'll make this marriage good —

together . . . For I know that it was meant. You to me were Heaven-sent — We'll be happy and content — together.

Our Dancing Years

It is only a melody recalled from long ago —
but it has the power to set my empty heart
aglow — with memories that go back to the
rich romantic past — when love was new and
life was good; so good — too good to last.

It is only a melody upon a record played — but
it fills the room with pictures that can never
fade — more vivid and more real than those
that hang upon the wall — How wonderful
that this small disc can resurrect it all — with
such a deep intensity — and bring you
laughing back to me — without the hurt,
without the tears — to live again our dancing
years.

The Summer of the Glory

Where did the summer go? Where, indeed? It went on the wings of the wind-wafted seed ... It went with the leaves that were loosed from the trees. It went with the petals that fell with the breeze.

The tale of the Jubilee summer is told — spelt out in glory of scarlet and gold ... A fairytale magic flashed over our lives — in a world dull and dreary romance still survives ... History here once again has been made — and memories planted that never will fade.

Peace, the Healer

I'm packing up my suitcase for a mini
holiday — near a little village, not so
very far away — and staying in a
cottage where the casements open wide
— upon a lane where wild flowers
clothe the banks on either side. A lane
too narrow for the monstrous
juggernauts to take — a lane so silent
you can hardly keep yourself awake.

I shall leave my problems and my
worries all behind — forgetting what
weighs heavily upon my troubled
mind . . . Minds as well as bodies need a
pause, to rest awhile — and rediscover
how to sleep, to think, to pray, to
smile . . . Peace, the finest tranquilliser,
calms the jangled brain — Peace that
falls around you like a soft and gentle
rain — Peace, the healer, needed in a
world where old and young — are
stretched beyond their bearing,
overwrought and overstrung.

Seeing in the Dark

Sometimes you see in the darkness — a thing that you missed in the light . . . The day with its trouble and turmoil — obscured what came clear in the night. As if someone, suddenly, somewhere — had flashed a great lamp in your way — revealing a truth that was hidden — as madly you rushed through the day.

Sometimes a thought like an angel comes whispering deep in the night — and gives you the clue you are seeking — so simple, so plain, and so right . . . Sometimes you're so busy looking at this and at that as you climb — you don't see the grand view unfolding, although it was there all the time.

Safely Moored

Safe and sturdy looks that little boat —
anchored there as if upon a pond — on waters
of tranquility to float — calm as if no wild sea
lay beyond — the quiet inlet where she lies
tonight — home before the fading of the light.

Tomorrow she will catch the morning tide —
and be tested whether stong or frail . . . We too
in this life are proved and tried. Some ride out
the storms and others fail — to reach the
haven of the harbour walls — safely moored
before the darkness falls.

Too Late Now

When you come we meet as friends — but
when you say goodbye — you leave a haunting
sadness like the echo of a sigh . . . Merry is the
laughter, gay the talk and bright the scene —
but underneath it all I hear the words: it might
have been.

Yes, indeed, it might have been. I see it in your
eyes. We might have loved each other once —
but things went otherwise . . . Life works out its
own designs, and we survive somehow. All is
for the best, they say. Too late for loving
now . . . Too late for disentangling the frayed
and twisted thread — too late to obliterate the
foolish words we said. For a different kind of
life the stage has now been set. Burden not the
present with the ashes of regret.

Meet Me Under the Clock

Meet me under the clock, you said. For that
was where we met — to keep our weekly
rendezvous. Some things you don't forget. I
kept the date. I saw you there — but where was
the station clock? Where it used to be there
hung a dial that seemed to mock — at my
romantic mood — for it was modern, bright
and cold — bleak, unfriendly, soul-less, and I
suddenly felt old.

We went into the restaurant. You smiled and
ordered tea — but everything fell flat for Time
had played a prank with me. The you I knew
just wasn't there, the you of twenty-one. Our
once dear dream lay dead between us. Life its
course had run . . . To think I'd wasted money
on a new blue hat and frock! It might have
been quite different if they hadn't changed the
clock.

The Last Lost Word

I wonder what it was you said — as I turned
and tossed my head — walking away into the
night — where the street lamps paled the
moon's white light . . . Was it the word that I
longed to hear? Too quickly I went as a car
drew near — and carried the sound of your
voice away. I might, if I'd waited, have heard
you say — the one lovely thing that I ached to
know . I was too hasty. You let me go.

I hoped you would follow. How proud we were!
How proud and how foolish it was to err —
thinking the worst and not the best — putting
our new love to the test. If only I'd waited the
truth to learn — our lives might have taken a
different turn.

Gardens Bring Back Memories

Gardens bring back memories, the thought of bygone hours — mingles with the present as you walk amongst your flowers ... They stir the recollection of some unforgotten place — and call to mind out of the past, a scene, a voice, a face.

Even when the last rose falls upon the frosted clay — you catch upon the wintry wind a song of yesterday. In every corner of the garden something you will see — that evokes within your heart some lovely memory.

Remember Them

When you're walking happily beneath a
shining sky — think of the afflicted and
of all condemned to lie —looking
through a windowpane at bird and
cloud and bloom — spending all the
golden moments shut up in a room.

All too often we forget when we are
young and strong — the old, the weary
and the weak and those who all day
long — lie within their prison walls and
never know the bliss — of feeling on
their brows, the wind's cool touch, the
sun's warm kiss.

Always Too Soon

Winter, oh winter, you've come here too
soon — I'm still in the mood for the
roses of June — and as for the Autumn
with leaves blowing bright — it flashed
past my door like a thief in the night.

Grey fall the evenings, so early, so drear
— plunging us down in the trough of
the year — but Nature knows best and
perhaps we all need — a time to reflect
before sowing new seed ... The
deepening darkness is warmed by a
thought — remembering all that the
good days have brought.

Time Will Bring it Back

No good deed is ever wasted and no kind word said in vain — for the good we do for others Life brings back to us again . . . Every seed of love you sow will spring up somewhere on the road — and the sacrifice you make will serve to lighten someone's load.

No good deed is lost to God although it may be lost to view. Cast your bread upon the waters. Time will bring it back to you.

Sitting in the Sunshine

In this cottage she was born and here lived as a wife. Here she raised a family and lived her long hard life — scrubbing, baking, proud and happy, caring for her own — loving every nook and corner, every stick and stone.

Now about the hearth there ring no voices young and gay. The children and their children's children; all have gone away ... Yet she's never lonely for she lives her life once more — as she sits there in the sunshine at the cottage door ... Hair like snow, back bent with age and finely crinkled brow — like the skin of wrinkled russets on the apple bough.